There goes Kafka!
Where is he going? Around Prague, his
ometown. Klaus Wagenbach, oldest Kafka hand
Eine Biographie seiner Jugend, *1957;* Kafka in
elbstzeugnissen, *1964;* In der Strafkolonie, *1975;*
ilder aus seinem Leben, *1983), went after him.*

*View from the Kleine to the Große Altstädter Ring, 1896:
on the left, the house Minuta, in the middle the Altstadt Town Hall Tower
with the Clock of the Apostles, at the back on the right the Teyn Church*

Kafka's Prague
A Travel Reader

Klaus Wagenbach

translated by Shaun Whiteside

THE OVERLOOK PRESS

WOODSTOCK • NEW YORK

914.3712
W

First published in 1996 by
The Overlook Press
Lewis Hollow Road
Woodstock, New York 12498

Library of Congress Cataloging-in-Publication Data

Wagenbach, Klaus.
[Kafkas Prag. English]
Kafka's Prague / Klaus Wagenbach.
p.   cm.
Translation of Kafkas Prag.
1. Kafka, Franz, 1883-1924—Homes and haunts—Czech Republic
—Prague. 2. Authors, Austrian—20th century—Biography.
3. Prague (Czech Republic)—Description and travel. I. Title
PT2621.A26Z982413   1996   883'.912—dc20   95-4331l4

Manufactured in Mexico
Type formatting by Bernard Schleifer
ISBN 0-87951-644-5
FIRST EDITION
10 9 8 7 6 5 4 3 2 1

Key to Text

All numbers shown in square brackets [1] in text refer to th
corresponding numbers in the endpaper maps: *front*, in German
back, in Czech.

All letters shown in square brackets [A] in text refer to the speci
maps reproduced in the appropriate chapter.

The places appear in **bold**, titles in *italics*.

Contents

Karlsbrücke/Charles Bridge with the Little Quarter bridge tower, around 1910

Preface

Franz Kafka, whose cool prose, sparse in vocabulary and yet "Kleistian" in tone, whose literary images—of the performing ape or the transformed Samsa, the country surveyor or the penal colony—and whose expert reports on power as it was to be exerted from the middle of our century has left such an enduring influence on almost all the world's literatures, hardly ever left his home city of Prague during his short life (1883-1924): several business trips, a number of educational visits, many stays in sanatoria, six months in Berlin, and a few months in the Bohemian countryside—nothing more.

"Prague," Kafka wrote as a nineteen-year-old, "doesn't let go. This little mother has claws." And in 1912, at the age of twenty-nine, with four years' work as a clerk behind him, and on the point of writing his first novel: How can I live in Prague! This yearning for people that I have, and which becomes fear when fulfilled, can only be assuaged in the holidays. . . ." Two years later in his diary: "Leave Prague. Counter this most powerful human injury that has ever befallen me with the strongest antidote at my disposal." And in 1917, with resignation: "Prague: Religions fade away like people."

So if you wish to know what houses Kafka lived in (almost all of them are still standing) or what he means when he writes: "I prefer to go strolling in parks and avenues," in short, what Kafka "had before his eyes," you must go to Prague, in reality or in the imagination. This travel book-cum-reader is intended as an accompaniment for both kinds of journey, and I have taken special care to show the houses and streets as they appeared in Kafka's lifetime.

In front of the Oppelthaus, 1920-21

Kafka's Prague

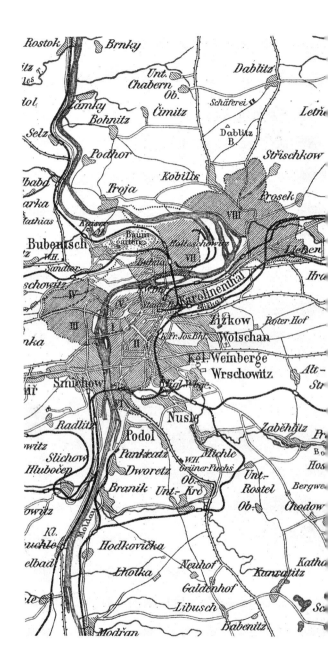

n Kafka's day (all the following details refer to the years round 1910), Prague, the "capital of the kingdom of Bohemia," was, after Vienna and Budapest, the third-largest city in the Austro-Hungarian monarchy under Kaiser Franz Joseph—230,000 inhabitants living in eight districts of the city. On the right of the River Moldau (Vltava) was the Old Town (Prague I), including the former Ghetto, the Josefov, or Josefstadt (Prague V), whose medieval buildings were razed between 1895 and 1905, and replaced by "modern tenement palaces." Next to the Old Town was the New Town (Prague II). On the other side of the Moldau was the Kleinseite, or "little quarter" (Prague III) and the area surrounding the Hradčany Castle (Prague IV); in about 1900 the areas of Vyšehrad, Hološevice-Bubna, and Lieben were added.

Of course the city had spread beyond these boundaries long before and, taking all its suburbs into account, had a population of over 600,000. In addition, the high levels of Czech immigration had turned it from a predominantly German to an almost purely Czech city, with a minority of 32,000 German speakers, more than half of them Jewish: "German Prague" was also a Jewish Prague. It was concentrated in the Old Town (population 36,000) and Josefov (population 4,000), with the result that German was predominantly spoken in the center, while Czech was spoken almost exclusively in the rest of the city. The "Prague German" spoken in this island (the nearest cohesive German-speaking area was some 30 miles away) was a dialect-free, low-vocabulary *Schriftdeutsch* (standard German): Kafka wrote in this another tongue and rarely lived and worked anywhere other than in this central district of Prague.

Egon Erwin Kisch described the Prague Germans: "Almost to a man they were upper-class, owners of the brown-coal mines, administrators in the coal and steel industry and the Škoda armaments factory, hop traders who traveled back and forth between Saaz and North America, sugar, textile, and paper manufacturers and bank managers;

they socialized with professors, high-class officers and city officials. There was barely such a thing as a German proletariat. The Germans, only five percent of Prague's population, had two magnificent theaters, an enormous concert hall, two colleges, four *Gymnasien* and four secondary schools, two daily newspapers with morning and evening editions, large clubhouses and a lively social life."

The two "magnificent theaters" were what was later to be the Deutsche Landestheater, built in 1781, and the Neue Deutsche Theater (see p. 109), opened in 1888 which seated a total of 3,400 people. The "enormous concert hall" was the Rudolfinum (see p. 114), opened in 1882, the "two colleges" were the University and the Technical College, each divided into a German and a Czech section; there were 12,000 students at all four institutions, including just 2,000 at the German colleges. The "two daily newspapers" were the conservative, bourgeois *Bohemia* and the liberal *Prager Tagblatt.* When he wrote "large clubhouses," what he chiefly had in mind was the Deutsche Haus, an extensive complex with a number of restaurants, halls, and club rooms for a total of 232 (!) German associations.

Admittedly, this rich cultural life could hardly conceal the insecure political situation: the students, from the predominantly nationalist German Bohemian provinces, agitated against the liberal bourgeoisie, the workers against their capitalist exploiters, the Czechs against the economic and political dominance of the Germans. The most visible symbol of the Czech liberation movement was the 1891 "Bohemian National Exhibition" in the Baumgarten, for which the Observation Tower on the Laurenziberg hill (a copy of the Eiffel Tower in Paris) and two funicular railways were built; the last bilingual street signs disappeared in the same year. Since the nationalist "December unrests" of 1891, the Jews, who had hitherto been relatively unaffected, found themselves caught between the two sides, and from that point onward, as Theodor Herzl wrote, they struggled "to find their way, like a stowaway through the discord of nationalities."

The Hradčany, seen from Chotekstraße (Chotkova)

From the turn of the century until the First World War, Prague was governed almost entirely by emergency decree from Vienna, repeatedly interrupted by violent struggles for universal suffrage (introduced for men in 1907). In October 1918, the Czechoslovak Republic was proclaimed, with Prague as its capital.

Kafka experienced Prague as a deeply divided city: the (German) upper class—the aristocracy, the military, and industrialists—conservative, if not reactionary; the (Czech) lower class national democratic, if not nationalist; and in the middle the small, rather impotent liberal middle class (German, Jewish, and to a small extent Czech).

This difference, or we might say, this lack of synchronization, was all too tangible. Alongside the aristocratic barouches with liveried servants there drove the occasional automobile, manufactured in Reichenberg. The first large demonstrations, organized by the Social Democrats, involving up to 200,000 participants, strode past imperial pensioners wearing medals from the last Austro-Prussian War of 1866. Long after the introduction of the telephone (1895: a local call cost 20 hellers), there was still a toll of 2 hellers to be paid for crossing the Moldau bridges (with the exception of the Charles Bridge), and policemen with swords and plumed helmets would continue to ride on horseback past the new power station (1900) for two decades to come. By 1897 the first electric trams were in operation (ticket price: 14–30 hellers), covering a network approaching a hundred miles in length, and as a thirty-year-old Kafka still "enjoyed jumping from the tram," just as he liked to use the new "pneumatic post" (a tube dispatch system that had just been installed in the city center), to correspond with his friend Max Brod. The price was 45 hellers, or almost half a crown.

A lot of money for an articled clerk ("Concipist") in an insurance company, who had to get by on a daily wage of 11 crowns (320 crowns a month), and who might also have wished to go to the theater (an orchestra seat: 5 crowns) or to dine out in the evening (3 crowns). Or to

14

Emperor Franz Joseph in Prague, 1907

Electro-omnibus, 1907

Demonstration for suffrage

Tollhouse on the Kaiser-Franz-Brücke

ake the funicular railway to Petřin Hill (return journey: 24 hellers) including a trip up the Observation Tower (one crown) and a cup of coffee (25 hellers). Not to mention the *Sechser* (tip) for the doorman (20 hellers) if you came home after ten o'clock at night and the doorman had to open up. You had to consider whether you could afford a small apartment (monthly rent about 50 crowns, a larger one about 100 crowns), or whether it might not be better to continue to live with your parents until you were thirty-two). Not to mention the price of your beloved books, your own included: Kafka's first book, *Betrachtung* (*Contemplation*), 5 crowns 30 hellers in cloth covers, 7 crowns 60 hellers half-leather bound; *Die Verwandlung* ("The Metamorphosis") in the cheap pamphlet series *Der jüngste Tag*, one crown 90 hellers.

Franz Kafka, *The City Coat of Arms*

At first everything in the building of the Tower of Babylon was in fairly good order; indeed, the order might have been too great, too much thought was devoted to sign-posts, interpreters, lodgings for the workmen and communicating roads, as if they had centuries ahead of them to do the work. In fact, the prevailing opinion at that time was that one could not build slowly enough; with very little insistence, this opinion was enough to make one hesitate even to lay the foundations. The argument was as follows: The essential thing within the entire enterprise is the idea of building a tower that will reach to heaven. Compared to this idea everything else is trivial. The idea, once grasped in all its greatness, cannot disappear; as long as there are people there will also be the strong desire to complete the building of the tower. Given all this, however, one must not worry about the future; on the contrary, humanity's knowledge is increasing, architecture has made advances and will continue to make advances, a task that takes us a year may in a hundred years' time be accomplished in half a year, and done better, more enduringly. So why should one now exer oneself to the brink of one's powers? There would only be any sense in that if one could hope to build the tower in the course of a generation. But that was unthinkable. It was easier to imagine that the next generation, with its perfected knowledge, would find the previous generation's work bad and tea down what had been built, to begin all over again. Such idea paralyzed people's powers, and they devoted themselves less to the building of the tower than to the building of the city for the workmen. Each national group wanted to have the mos beautiful quarter, and arguments arose, intensifying to bloody conflicts. There was no end to these conflicts; to the leader they were a new argument in favor of the idea that the towe should, for want of concentration, be built either very slowly or, ideally, postponed until the universal declaration of peace So time was spent not only in conflict; in the intervals the tow was beautified, which sadly generated fresh envy and fresh conflicts. The age of the first generation passed in this fashion, bu none that followed was any different, except that technica accomplishment increased and so, in consequence, did the desire for conflict. In addition to this there was the fact that the second or third generation already recognized the senselessnes of building the tower to heaven, but by that time all the people were too involved with one another to leave the city All the legends and songs produced in that city were filled with longing for a prophesied day on which the city would be shattered by a quick succession of five blows from a huge fist And this is why the city has a fist in its coat of arms.

Kafka's life

About five years old

His father, Hermann Kafka
(1852-1931)

His mother, Julie Kafka, née
Löwy (1855-1934)

Kafka was born on July 3, 1883, the oldest child of the businessman Hermann Kafka and his wife, Julie, in Prague, on the boundary between the Old Town and the Josefstadt, at the edge of the Ghetto, which still existed as an architectural unit; his birthplace on the corner of Karpfengasse and Maiselgasse (Kaprova and Maiselova), with the old street number (the "conscription number") 27/1 was later redeveloped; only the gate remains.

His father, a butcher's son, had come to Prague a few years earlier from a small Jewish community in the provinces of South Bohemia as a poor traveling salesman, had married Julie Löwy, the daughter of a fairly prosperous brewer, and set himself up with growing success as a seller of "fancy goods" (walking sticks, umbrellas, threads, fashion accessories, haberdashery). During the first few years the family moved several times, as they rose socially and economically.

From 1889 until 1896, they had their first fairly long stay in a house ("Minuta") in which Kafka's sisters were also born. The child was brought up according to the rules prevailing among the upwardly mobile middle classes, by a governess, maidservants, and a cook. His parents spent the day in the shop, where his father was domineering boss; in the evening they had a late meal and then played their habitual game of cards.

From 1893 until 1901 Kafka attended the Staatsgymnasium mit deutscher Unterrichtssprache, or Deutsch Gymnasium, in Prague Altstadt, a humanist grammar school that did not teach art, music, or modern languages (Kafka learned French and later some English and Italian on his own initiative). He was seen as a modest, reticent pupil with average results (although his marks in mathematics were invariably dreadful). In 1896 the family moved to Zu den Drei Königen (At the Three Kings, a stone's throw from Minuta and the Gymnasium), a building which would later house his father's haberdashery.

After his *Abitur*, or "leaving certificate," in 1901, Kafka initially planned to study German literature, but then opted for law, a subject which, along with medicine, offered the best employment opportunities for Jews. His father seemed to have come to terms with the fact that his son was not going to be a businessman—in doing so he was following (as Kafka put it in the "Letter to His Father") "what you took as your standard, the universal way of treating sons among the Jewish middle class, or at least the value judgments of that class."

For his son it was still merely the tiresome choice of a bread-and-butter job that would leave writing (already his "main yearning") as unhampered as possible. He completed his course in law at the German Karl Ferdinand University in Prague, where, "along with copious quantities of nerves, [he] nourished himself on sawdust that had already been chewed by a thousand mouths," and completed the course in the shortest possible period of eight terms.

Abitur *photograph, 1901*

Graduation photograph, 1906

During his time at university Kafka was a member of the Reading and Debating Group of German Students in Prague, where he met his lifelong friend, Max Brod. He wrote his earliest surviving prose piece, "Description of a Struggle."

After graduating and undergoing the obligatory *Gerichtsjahr* (the year that law graduates spent being initiated into court procedure), Kafka worked, thanks to an uncle, first in the Prague branch of the insurance company Assicurazioni Generali, which he left a year later to work for the Workers' Accident Insurance Institute of the Kingdom of Bohemia in Prague, in whose large office building he accomplished his daily duties until his retirement.

The working day was considerably shorter than it had been in Assicurazioni Generali. There he had had to work eleven to twelve hours a day, while here he worked only six and a half. In the new job he had to work Saturdays as well, however, which meant that—with only fourteen days' vacation—Kafka worked longer hours than an insurance clerk today. However, the afternoons or evenings were devoted to long walks "back and forth through the city, across the Hradcin, around the Cathedral, and across the Belvedere." Or to attend political meetings by the Social Democrats, the Realists (the party of the future state founder, Masaryk), and anarchists. Or to participate in the discussion group devoted to the philosophy of Franz Brentano at the Café Louvre and evenings of lectures in the hospitable salon of the pharmacist's wife Berta Fanta, about the most up-to-date themes of the day: quantum theory, psychoanalysis, the theory of relativity.

The theater he visited most often during this time was a "flea-pit" in the Café Savoy on Ziegenplatz (Vitězná); a "lingo troupe" from Poland performing Yiddish plays. It was his first encounter with living (Eastern) Jewry, the traces of which are still apparent in his late work.

Even if his son had no desire to become a businessman, in 1911 Hermann Kafka made one final attempt at least to familiarize him with the world of business. He gave him a share in his son-in-law's factory, which Kafka was to take care of. This led to violent arguments, and on two occasions even to thoughts of suicide: "I stood at the window for a very long time, and it would often have given me pleasure to startle the toll collector on the bridge by falling." At this time (October 1912) the family was living in one of the new apartment blocks in Josefstadt, at the end of Niklasstrasse (Mikulášská), with view of the also newly built Čechův Bridge and that same toll collector.

Shortly before this—in a single night—he had written his first great "story," "The Judgment", and a short time before that, at the home of Max Brod, Kafka had met "the Berliner," later to be his fiancée, Felice Bauer, to whom he dedicated "The Judgment." In the same year he wrote "The Metamorphosis" and large parts of *Der Verschollene* (*Amerika*), and at the end of this fruitful year he published his first book, *Meditation*.

At this time, in a letter to his fiancée, Kafka describes his daily routine:

From 8 till 2 or 2:20 office, until 3 or 3:30 lunch, from then on sleeping in bed (usually just trying to, for a week in that sleep I saw nothing but Montenegrins with an extremely disagreeable, headache-inducing clarity of each detail of their complicated costume) until 7:30, then 10 minutes exercise, naked at the open window, then an hour walking alone or with Max or with some other friend, then dinner with my family, then at 10:30 (although it's often as late as 11:30), sit down to write and stay at it according to strength, pleasure, and happiness until 1, 2, 3 in the morning.

With the growing flood of letters to Felice (over three hundred letters in the first eleven months of their correspondence), his literary productivity began to run dry, a period that Kafka saw as an alternative between "life" (meaning life with Felice) and "writing," culminating in a first engagement in June 1914, which was broken off four weeks later: Kafka opted for writing.

During the first months of the war he began work on *The Trial* and wrote "In the Penal Colony" (which was

t the age of about thirty-six, around 1920

ot published until 1919)—first of all in apartments lent im by his sisters, and later in his own apartments away om the house of his parents, who had moved to the lux- rious Oppelthaus in November 1913. During these ears he produced three more books: *The Stoker* (1913), *he Metamorphosis* (1915), *The Judgment* (1916).

But the temptation of the "life" that he so admired and ·ared remained, even in "temporary measures" such as egetarian food, working in a nursery at the Pomological istitute, or staying in natural cure sanatoria. A visit to 1arienbad with Felice in the summer of 1916 brought ·conciliation, and his productivity resumed, particularly ·rompted by the opportunity to write in a cottage that is sister Ottla rented near to Prague Castle, and from

March 1917 in a new apartment of his own in the Schönborn Palace beneath the Castle. It was in these two apartments that he wrote almost all the stories in *A Country Doctor*, published in 1920. In August 1917, a few weeks after his second engagement to Felice, he developed the "illness that had for years been heralded by headlessness and sleeplessness," the "coughing of blood" which Kafka called "almost a relief."

The onset of pulmonary tuberculosis freed Kafka from all his duties. For six months he lived with his sister Ottla in a Bohemian village, but then, as was to occur a number of times, he had to return to his job in the Workers Insurance Institute, repeatedly interrupted by periods spent in sanatoria, until he finally retired in the summer of 1922. In the meantime he returned to live with his parents in the Oppelthaus in Prague, where parts of the novel *The Castle* and some of the late stories were written. All the other "escape attempts"—another engagement, to Julie Wohryzek, his love for Milena Jesenská, life in Berlin with Dora Diamant—failed. Kafka died on June 3, 1924, and was buried in the Jewish Cemetery in Straschnitz (Olšany), in Prague, the city he hated and could not leave, which held him captive and whose diversity and strangeness he captured in his writings.

A few weeks after his death his seventh and last book was published, the collection of stories entitled *A Hunger Artist*.

The Houses

His birthplace

South side of the Große Altstädter Ring, with the Marian Column (destroyed at the end of the war).

On the right the entrance to the Eisengasse, his mother lived in the corner house (Smetanahaus) before she was married. In the third house from the right, the Unicorn Pharmacy, was Bertha Fanta's literary salon (see p. 25), the sixth house along, by the entrance to the Zeltnergasse, is the Sixthaus

About two years old

Birthplace

For a short time there has been a little Kafka exhibition, in his **birthplace** [1] what is now No. 5 Rathausgasse (U radnice), of which only the portal remains, and on the facade there is a memorial bust erected during the "Prague Spring" of the mid-sixties.

Between 1885 and 1888 the family moved three times, and the houses have since been torn down: No. 56 Wenzelsplatz (Václavské náměstí), 7/187 Geistgasse (Dušní ulice), No. 6 Niklasstrasse (Mikulášská)—the latter two in the ghetto, later redeveloped. The ghetto, as Kafka knew it in his youth, has been preserved in a beautiful wooden model by Anton Langweil (1826-34, in the Prague Museum).

Sixthaus

The first family house that can still be visited is their fifth, where they lived from August 1888 until May 1889: the **Sixthaus** [2] (dated 1796 above the door, but built earlier), No. 2 Zeltnergasse (U Celetná), the first house on the right as one approaches from the Großer Ring (Na Příkopě).

Minuta

From June 1889 until September 1896, the family lived in the house **Minuta** (or: **Minutta**) [3], another old (17th century) house, which divides the Großer and the Kleiner Altstädter Ring, No. 2 Kleiner Ring (Malé náměstí); the *sgraffiti* were still painted over at that time. It was here, after two brothers had died in infancy ("through the fault of the doctors"), that Kafka's three sisters were born: Elli (1889), Valli (1890), and Ottla (1892, "my favorite," he writes).

His sisters, from the left: Elli, Valli, Ottla

Today there is a café on the ground floor. Through the main entrance, which leads to the magistrates' court, one reaches the inner courtyard, ringed around by *Pawlatschen* (from the Italian *Parvola loggia*), the balconies typical of Old Prague. It was on one of these *Pawlatschen* that Kafka's father demonstrated the method of bringing up children of which his son later complained about in "Letter to His Father":

Today, of course, I cannot directly describe your upbringing techniques during my very first years, but I can more or less imagine them by drawing conclusions from my later years. . .

The Minuta house, around 1900

All I remember directly is an event from my first years. You may remember it as well. I was once persistently whining for water in the night, certainly not out of thirst, but probably partly to annoy, partly to entertain myself. After some strong threats had been to no avail, you took me from my bed, carried me onto the balcony and left me standing there alone at the locked door for a while, standing in my nightshirt. I don't mean that this was unjust, perhaps there really was no other way of achieving a quiet night, but I do wish to use it to characterize your educational methods and the effect they had on me. Even years later I suffered from the painful notion that the gigantic man, my father, the ultimate authority, could come for me, almost groundlessly, and carry me from my bed to the balcony, and that I was therefore, for him, a mere nonentity.

He had been "a dependent creature" as a child, Kafka noted in his diary, and indeed he had been, alone with the nurse or the cook, separated from the oldest sister by six years, from the youngest by nine. Playing with neighbors' children, left alone "in the street," was hardly the done thing. His parents rarely ever saw their child throughout the day, and seldom in the evening; they were parents for outings and holidays.

In Haus Minuta he was once given a *Sechser*. A Sechser was a 10-kreuzer piece (before 1900 they still used kreuzers and guilders). What happened next, Kafka tells his friend Milena thirty years later:

Once as a very small boy I got a Sechser and had a strong desire to give it to an old beggar woman who was sitting between the Großer and the Kleiner Ring. But now the sum seemed enormous to me, a sum that had probably never been given to a beggar, and so I was ashamed to do something so monstrous to a beggar woman. But I had to give it to her, so I got change for the Sechser, gave the beggar woman a kreuzer, ran around the whole complex of the City Hall and the avenue on the Kleiner Ring, came out again as an entirely new benefactor, gave the beggar woman a kreuzer again, began to run, and happily did this ten times (or rather less, because I think the beggar woman later lost her patience and disappeared on me). Anyway, at the end, morally too, I was so exhausted that I ran straight home and cried until my mother replaced the Sechser.

t the Three Kings

he family moved into the very old and essentially late-
othic house **At the Three Kings** [5] at No. 3
eltnergasse (U Celetná) in September 1896, with the
eginning of Kafka's fourth Gymnasium class, and lived
ere until June 1907, during his years as a student and
most the whole of the *Gerichtsjahr* that followed
aduation.

The family's apartment was on the first floor. For
ecades afterward (until the collapse of Communism),
ese rooms were occupied by a vegetarian restaurant
at Kafka, who became a vegetarian after his thirtieth
rthday or thereabouts, would certainly have visited, at
ast in the evening, because "for months my father had
 hold the newspaper in front of his face during my sup-
er before he got used to it." Before, that is, he got used
: "yogurt, granary bread, all kinds of nuts, chestnuts,
ates, figs, grapes, almonds, raisins, squashes, bananas,
oples, pears, oranges. Everything eaten in groups, of
ourse, and not piled into me like a cornucopia."

In this apartment, much to the envy of his classmates,
afka also had, for the first time, a room of his own, with
window overlooking the street (and not, as many guides
ave it, with a window overlooking the Teyn Church).
Ve have a description of his room by a member of the
omestic staff: "His room was simply decorated. Next to
e door was a desk, and on it the *Roman Law* in two vol-
mes. Opposite the window was a closet, in front of it a
icycle, then the bed, next to the bed a little bedside
ble, and by the door a bookshelf and a wash basin."

We also have an account that Kafka wrote to a girl-
iend about the "first night":

Ve were living in the Zeltnergasse at the time. There was
 clothes shop opposite, where a shopgirl used to stand in the
oorway, and upstairs I, a little over twenty years old, paced
cessantly up and down, engrossed in the nerve-racking busi-
ess of cramming meaningless facts for my first state exam. It
as very hot, very hot, it was quite unbearable, I kept stopping

Stairs in the house At the Three Kings

by the window, the repulsive history of Roman law betwee
my teeth, and finally we made an arrangement by sign lan
guage. I was to collect her in the evening at eight o'clock, b
when I came down in the evening there was already someon
else there, although that didn't make much difference, I w
afraid of the whole world, and therefore of this man as we
even if he hadn't been there I would still have been afraid
him. But although the girl took his arm, she still gestured to n
to walk behind them. We duly arrived at Schützen Island, dran
some beer there, with me sitting at the next table, and then w
walked, with me behind, slowly to the girl's apartment, some
where near the Fleischmarkt, there the man said good-bye, th
girl ran into the house, I waited for a while until she came bac
out to me, and then we went to a hotel on the Kleinseite.

It was also in the house in Zeltnergasse that Kafka, wh
had already begun to write at the Gymnasium, wrote h
first texts. He later destroyed almost all of them. Only
few were collected in the first book; one of these excep
tions is *The Window on the Street*.

The house At the Three Kings in the Zeltnergasse

Franz Kafka, *The Window on the Street*

Anyone who leads a solitary life and yet wishes now and the to have some kind of contact, anyone who, according t changes of the time of day, the weather, working conditior and so on, simply wants to see any arm at all that he could clin to—he will not get by for long without a window on th street. And if he is not in the mood of wanting anything, an simply walks to the windowsill a tired man, his eyes movin between his audience and the heavens, not wanting to look ou and tilting his head back a little, the horses below will swee him away in their wake of carts and noise and thus, at last, int the human harmony.

Passport photograph as a schoolboy,
about sixteen years old

The "Shop"

His parents' marriage and the establishment of their business coincided both in time (1882) and in place: It was in the building on the north side of the Altstädter Ring (Staroměstské náměstí), where they had celebrated their marriage (**Hotel Goldhammer**), that Hermann Kafka founded his fancy-goods shop, initially as a high-street retail store. All that remains of this building is a painting (see page 72) and a description of his father's disputes by his son (in "Letter to His Father"):

The shop. In fact, particularly as a child, while it was a mainstreet shop, I would have been glad, it was so lively, lit in the evening, one could see and hear a great deal, one could help here and there, distinguish oneself, but above all admire you, with all your splendid business talents. . . . But as for me, I saw and heard you shouting, raging, ranting and raging in the shop, something which, as I thought at the time, was unique in the whole world. And not just raging, but other kinds of tyranny as well. Like the way you took goods that you didn't want people to confuse with different ones, and hurled them from the counter. . . . Or the expression you always used about a trainee with lung disease: "He should die, the sick dog." You called the employees "paid enemies," and that's what they were, but even before they had become so, you seemed to me to be their "paying enemy."

It appears that the shop remained unharmed throughout the Czech nationalist, anti-Semitic "December unrests" in 1891, as Hermann Kafka was thought—not entirely without reason—to be a Czech. One who, when he moved the shop to the house At the Three Kings [5] in September 1896, became a "sworn expert witness" to the Trade Court, with his own telephone. The mainstreet retail store made way for a wholesale store, the family went on living in the same house (see p. 35), and the oldest son had his own room.

HERRMANN KAFKA, PRAG I.

Zeltnergasse 3.

Galanteriewaren en gros Geschäft.

No. 12 Zeltnergasse

The Kinsky Palais on the Altstädter Ring
On the ground floor on the right is Herrmann Kafka's shop.

Ten years later, the room was too small, and in May 906 the shop moved to the first floor of the building iagonally opposite, at 12 Zeltnergasse [6] (Celetná), /here it remained until 1912.

The 19th-century house is still in good condition, ith a beautiful *fin-de-siècle* staircase and a *Pawlatsche*)alconied) courtyard.

1 1912 his father's business moved to the right wing of ie lavish Kinsky Palace on the Altstädter Ring, in the :nement of which Kafka had been a pupil at the the .ltstadt Gymnasium (see p. 71). But before this, in)ctober 1907, when Kafka began his job as an assistant : Assicurazioni Generali (see p. 77), he was recommend- :d in a document: "He comes from a respected family."

ake the path between Hermann Kafka's four businesses: iey are barely one hundred yards apart. The father's :ographical world was even more limited than his son's.

HERMANN KAFKA
PRAG I.,
ALTSTADTERRING No. 16
Palais Kinsky.

GALANTERIEWAREN EN GROS.

Sachverständiger des k. k. Landes- als Strafgerichtes.

Postsparkassen-Konto No. 2.131.
TELEFON No. 141.

'is father's letterhead (1918). At the bottom is the iblem, the jackdaw (Czech: kavka), which was 'merly hopping on an oak tree (right). Similarly, 'anz's father changed the spelling of his given name 'er time: Hermann, Herrmann, Heřman.

At the Ship; the Civilian Swimming School

The Kafka family's move in June 1907 from the mediev.
house **At the Three Kings** [5] to the house **At th**
Ship [11], 36 Niklasstrasse (Mikulášská), an apartmer
house rebuilt after the redevelopment of the Jewish quar
ter, definitively marks their social rise. It was a new builc
ing with an elevator; the family lived on the top floo
with a view of the Moldau and the Rudolfinum. In fror
of the house, for only the next five years, was a "bi
empty building site," the Johannesplatz. And the bridg
over the Moldau, the Čech Bridge, was still being bui
when Kafka moved in, so he called Niklasstrasse
"Suicide Approach," because it "leads to the river, wher
a bridge is being built, and the Belvedere on the oppc

The Čech Bridge in the year in which it was built, 1908
The new apartment block on the left at the entrance to Niklasstraße,
with a tram driving past: the house At the Ship

ite bank, hills and gardens, will have a tunnel built
underneath, so that you can walk down the street over
he bridge, and go for a walk under the Belvedere." Kafka
would later do precisely that, and it became one of his
favorite walks (see p. 96).

Kafka described his room quite often, for example in
his diary, lying on the sofa in the evening darkness:

The lights and shadows cast by the electric light on the street
and the bridge down on the walls and ceiling are irregular....
With the installation of the electric arc lamps down below, and
the decoration of this room, no housewifely care was taken as
to how my room, at this hour and without its own illumina-
tion, would look from the couch.

In this room, during the famous night of his literary "breakthrough," between the September 22 and 23 1912 ("from ten o'clock in the evening until six o'clock in the morning"), Kafka wrote his first great short story "The Judgment"—at the end of which Georg Bendemann swings over the balustrade of a bridge, "Still clutching on with weakening grip, he glimpsed a bu through the bars of the balustrade, and knew that i would easily mask the sound of his fall. . . ."

A few weeks later he wrote "The Metamorphosis," and large sections of the "American" novel *Der Verschollen* (*Amerika*) were written in the room on Niklasstrasse Kafka also captured the view from his room:

The view of staircases moves me so today. A long time ago, and several times since, I delighted in the triangular detail, visible from my window, of the steps that lead on the right from the Čech Bridge down to the Quai Plateau. Very sloping, as though dropping a rapid hint. And now, across the river, I can see a steep flight of steps on the embankment that leads to the water It has always been there, but is revealed in the autumn and winter by the removal of the swimming school that is otherwise there, and lies there in the dark grass beneath the brown tree in the play of perspective.

Kafka was, incidentally, a keen user of this **Civilian Swimming School** [15], founded in 1840, and so called to distinguish it from the Military Swimming School rather higher up; he had his own boat there (a "leaky old tub"). The long building can still be seen today.

Niklasstrasse is now called Pařižká třída. The house **At the Ship** no longer exists, and in its place stands the Hotel Praha-Intercontinental. Anyone wishing to follow Kafka's gaze can still do this: from a window in the Intercontinental restaurant on the top floor.

[German handwritten manuscript text]

Beginning of the manuscript of "The Judgment" in his diary

The "Civilian Swimming School" on the Vltava in the background the "Military Swimming School"

Max Brod's Apartment

Kafka's lifelong friend Max Brod (1884-1968), who rescued Kafka's posthumous work, lived in the top story of the house at 1 **Schalengasse** [19] (Skořepka), until his marriage (1913, then 8 Ufergasse/Břehová). At that time he was working in the post office, and used to wait for the insurance official Kafka after work on Josefsplatz, to walk with him.

In this house Kafka read his friend his works, which he had often just completed, and it was here too that he first met his future fiancée Felice Bauer. In his 1912 diary he writes:

Miss Felice Bauer. When I arrived at Brod's on August 13 she was sitting at the table, and struck me as looking like a serving wench. I was not at all curious about who she was, but immediately took her for granted. Bony, empty face that wore its emptiness openly. Bare neck. Blouse thrown on. She looked very domestic in her clothes, although, as it later turned out, she was no such thing. . . . Broken-looking nose. Blonde, rather stiff, unattractive hair, strong chin. While I was sitting down took a closer look at her for the first time, and by the time was seated I had already formed an unshakable opinion.

Max Brod
Drawing by Lucien Bernhard

Max Brod's apartment in the Schalengasse

Felice Bauer, 1914

Oppelthaus

In November 1913 the family moved to the house on the corner of Pariser Strasse (Pařižká třída) and Altstädter Ring (Staroměstské náměstí), the **Oppelthaus** [21]. The postal address was 6 (now 5) Altstädter Ring. The Oppelthaus was one of the apartment buildings erected after redevelopment: a four-story luxury house with oriel windows, an elevator, an added mezzanine, and a tall roof with a corner tower.

The family's six-room apartment, bigger and more luxurious than the one in the house **At the Ship** (see p. 42), was in the corner of the third floor. Kafka's room overlooked Pariser Strasse:

Right outside my window I have the big dome of the Russian Church [Church of St. Nicholas] with two towers and between the dome and the nearest apartment building a view of the little triangular section of the Laurenziberg with a very small church. On the left I can see the Rathaus with the tower rising sharply with all its great mass, and reclining again in a perspective that no one else, perhaps, has seen properly before.

Kafka lived here until the end of July 1914, and then again from 1918 (see p. 65).

When part of the City Hall was destroyed in 1945, the Oppelthaus was also damaged. The roof is new, the mezzanine floor is gone; but the Kafkas' apartment is still standing. The original doorway with the two columns (5 Altstädter Ring) no longer leads to the old staircase. On the other hand, the next-door entrance (No. 6) has a fine city coat-of-arms, and if you want to take a look at the courtyard of the building, you can do so through the entrance at No. 4 Pařižká třída.

View of the Niklas-(Pariser)-Straße
On the left the Altstadt Town Hall, on the right the Oppelthaus

Altstädter Ring
On the left the Niklaskirche (Church of St. Nicholas),
on the right the Oppelthaus

Bilekgasse

At the age of thirty-one, Kafka lived alone for the first time, in the corner house on Bilekgasse [22] (Bílkova) first from August 3, 1914, for about four weeks as a guest in the apartment of his sister Valli, and then again in a different apartment in the same building from February 10 until March 15, 1915, when he was the chief tenant.

His decision in favor of a room of his own was not entirely voluntary. On July 31, 1914, his two brothers-in-law Karl Hermann (husband of his sister Elli) and Josef Pollak (husband of his sister Valli) were called up to the army; Elli, with two small children, moved in with her parents in the Oppelthaus (see p. 48), and the bachelor Franz had to move.

Kafka, who had barely written anything in the previous two years, and who had broken up with his fiancé Felice Bauer a few weeks previously, contemplated the general belligerence full "of envy and hatred for the combatants, whom I passionately wish all ill." After a few days in Bilekgasse, he began work on *The Trial*, first writing the opening and closing chapters, and then at least two more chapters.

After his sister Valli's return from vacation, Kafka moved to his sister Elli's empty apartment in **Nerudagasse** (see p. 52).

The building is still in good condition, with a beautiful internal staircase and skylight. Kafka's study was probably on the first floor, because he writes that it was "lower than my room" in the Oppelthaus, and that he was disturbed by the "choral singing from the inn opposite."

The room that Kafka rented in February 1915 was little higher up. It was probably here that he wrote "Blumfeld, an Elderly Bachelor." After a few weeks, however, Kafka gave up the room—his neighbor was too noisy, the landlady too quiet, someone was learning French in the next room. . . . He moved to the house **Zum goldenen Hecht** (At the Golden Pike) (see p. 57).

The house in Bilekgasse

The stairwell

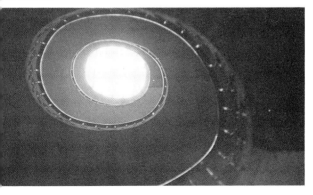

Nerudagasse; the Asbestos Factory

After Kafka had to move out of his sister Valli's apartment
in the **Bilekgasse** (see p. 50), he lived from the beginning
of September 1914 until February 9, 1915, in the apartment of his sister Elli, who had moved to her parents' in
the first months of the war. Elli's husband, Karl Hermann,
was the "industrialist" of the family: After his marriage to
Elli, he founded the Prague Asbestos Works Hermann &
Co.; the "Co." was Franz Kafka, with a stake from his
father.

The Hermann family's apartment was in the newly
built area of the district of Vinohrady, at **48 Nerudagasse**
(today: Polská). On the above map: [A]. From this apartment Kafka writes in a letter:

Unless something particular, especially the factory, disturbs me,
my timetable is as follows: Office until 2:20, then lunch at
home, then 1 or 2 hours reading newspapers, writing letters or
doing office work, then up to my apartment and sleep or just
lie awake, then at 9 down to my parents for supper (good
walk), back at 10 on the tram, and then stay awake as long as
my strength or fear of next morning, fear of headaches in the
office allow.

I sit or lie during the hours of the day, which are the only
ones I consider appropriate to my life, alone in these 3 quiet
rooms, I never come into contact with anyone, not even my
friends, just with Max for a few minutes on the way home from
the office.

he house in Nerudagasse

Karl Hermann with his wife
Elli, Kafka's sister
In front of them: Kafka's parents,
with grandson Felix

Hermann & Co. Prague Asbestos Works

Prague Factory, 1913

His brother-in-law's factory was quite close by, and in fact it did disturb Kafka because his father still clearly wanted to see him in the role of an industrialist. What had brought Kafka to the brink of suicide in October 1912 now repeated itself two years later when, (as his brother-in-law was a soldier, he often had to look after the factory, in the middle of writing *The Trial*. Thoughts of "suicide," despair about the "collapsing factory," the "wretched factory," "my father's reproaches," his own "worthless work."

And finally in January 1915: "As long as I have to go to the factory, I will not be able to write a thing." It was the end of *The Trial*, which remained a fragment.

However, the few months in Elli's apartment were an unusually fruitful period: He produced not only two thirds of *The Trial* (including the famous parable "Before the Law"), but also the "Oklahoma" chapter of *Der Verschollene* and the short story "In the Penal Colony."

The Prague asbestos works were in the courtyard of the house at **27 Borivogasse** (Bořivojova) [B], only a hundred yards away, but already in the workers' district of Žižkov. At its peak it employed twenty-five workers on fourteen machines driven by a gas motor with transmission belts; it was liquidated in 1917.

Today the house on Nerudagasse can no longer be reached by tram, only by subway (station: Jiřího z Poděbrad on Line A). Evidently the Hermann family had moved into the house in 1910 around the time of its completion. It was, like the whole area, designed (without an elevator) for the upper middle class, quite distinct from the working-class district of Žižkov, where the factory was. You can walk down the path, the few hundred yards that took the middle-class official to the two-story barracks of the courtyard factory (although it is also accessible by a rather wider passageway at No. 29 Ondříčkova).

And then take a walk in Kafka's beloved **Riegerpark (Riegrovy sady)** [C].

A Sunday walk in the Riegerpark, 1916

At the Golden Pike

Driven out by the noise at the **Bilekgasse** (see p. 50), on March 15, 1915, Kafka found an apartment in the building **Zum goldenen Hecht** [23] at 16 (formerly 8) Lange Gasse (Dlouhá), another newly built apartment block in Josefstadt. He lived there until February 28, 1918. Writing to his former fiancée Felice Bauer, with whom he was once again corresponding, he said in March 1915:

I've moved, to a room which is about ten times noisier than the previous one, but incomparably more beautiful in every other way. I had thought the situation and appearance of the room were irrelevant to me. But they are not. Without a relatively open view, without the chance of being able to see a large piece of sky from the window and a tower in the distance, say, if it cannot be open countryside, without this I am a wretched, oppressed man, I cannot tell you the precise amount of misery that attaches to the room, but it cannot be small; I even have the morning sun in the room, and as there are much lower roofs all around it comes fully and directly to me. But I don't get just the morning sun, because it is a corner room and two windows face southwest. But lest I become presumptuous, someone above me in a studio (empty, unrented!!) tramps up and down in heavy boots until evening, and has set up a redundant noise machine that sounds like a game of skittles.

A few days later the riddle of the "game of skittles" was solved, but Kafka still lamented the

resonance of the whole infernal concrete building. Above my room the machinery of the elevator purrs and echoes through the empty attic rooms. (That is what I took to be the studio ghost, but there are also serving-girls there, who, when they are drying the laundry, practically run their slippers over my scalp.)

The "more open view" from the balcony included that of an apartment with "morning sun in all three windows on to the street," diagonally opposite on the fourth floor, No. 5 Lange Gasse: it was the apartment he had chosen for himself and Felice to live in after their marriage.

As far as we can tell, hardly anything was written in A
the Golden Pike. Kafka's room was in the front of th
house on the fourth floor, his balcony is adorned wit
the coat-of-arms of the golden pike, the two window
looked out over the Fleischmarktgasse (Masná). Th
elevator is still in operation. . . .

The house At the Golden Pike
On the right Fleischmarktgasse, on the left the Lange Gasse

lchimistengasse

y the summer of 1916, tormented by the noise in the
artment in **At the Golden Pike** (see p. 57), Kafka had
least begun to look for a place to write at night, and
und it with his sister Ottla on Hradčany, the bailey of
rague Castle, in a little medieval cottage at 22
lchimistengasse [24] (Zlatá ulička):

ne day last summer I went with Ottla to look for a place to
e; I no longer believed in the possibility of real peace, but I
evertheless went looking. . . . Nothing, we found nothing suit–
le. For fun we made inquiries in the little alley. Yes, there
ould be a small house to let in November. Ottla, who is also
search of peace, in her own way, fell in love with the idea of
nting the house. . . .

e Alchimistengasse on Hradčany, Ottla's house on the left

It had many defects to begin with.... Today it suits m
completely. In every way: the agreeable walk up to it, th
silence there; I'm separated from a neighbor by only
very thin wall, but the neighbor is quiet enough; I tak
my supper up there and usually stay there until midnigh
then the advantage of the walk home: I have to resolve t
stop, and then I have the walk, which cools my head. An
the life there: It is something special to have a house o
one's own, to keep the world out by locking the door no
of the room, not of the apartment, but of the house itsel
to step from the door of the apartment straight into th
snow of the quiet street. The whole thing costs twent
crowns a month, my sister supplies all my needs, the li
tle flower-girl (Ottla's pupil) waiting on me as little a
possible, everything orderly and pleasant.

From the end of November 1916, Kafka wrote man
of his finest works here: "A Country Doctor," "In th
Gallery," "Gracchus the Hunter," "A Report to a
Academy," "The Anxieties of the Family Man." And als
"An Imperial Message"—obviously prompted in som
way by the imperial castle (and written shortly afte
the death of the Kaiser Franz Joseph), but probably i
memory of the legal foundation of the workers' acciden
insurance provision, Wilhelm II's "Imperial Message
proclaimed thirty years previously in Berlin, on th
"healing of social injuries."

The Alchimistengasse can be reached within the cast
walls via Georgsgasse (Jiřská ulice); today, far from bein
a "quiet street," it is a tourist attraction. Toward evenin
however, one can peacefully follow the walk that Kafk
took in the winter of 1916-17: "pleasant to walk hom
around midnight along the old castle steps down to th
city."

ranz Kafka, *An Imperial Message*

he emperor—it is said—has sent you, the individual, the
retched subject, the tiny shadow fleeing to the remotest dis-
nce in the face of the imperial sun, the emperor has, from his
eathbed, sent a message specifically to you. He made the mes-
nger kneel by the bed and whispered the message in his ear;
concerned about it was he that he had him repeat it into his
r. He confirmed the correctness of what was said with a nod
the head. And in the presence of all those who witnessed his
ath—all the obstructive walls are being demolished and on
e wide, soaring staircase the worthies of the empire stand in
circle—in the presence of all of them he dispatched the mes-
nger. The messenger set off straight away; a strong, tireless
an; outstretching now this arm, now that, he makes his way
rough the crowd; whenever he encounters resistance he
ints to his chest, with the sign of the sun; and he advances
ith ease, like no other. But the crowd is so great; their
vellings are endless. If the open countryside opened up, how
would fly, and soon you would hear the wonderful beats of
fists on your door. But instead, how uselessly he exerts him-
lf; he is still forcing his way through the chambers of the
nermost depth of the palace; he will never overcome them;
d if he did so, nothing would have been achieved; he would
ve to fight his way down the stairs; and if he managed this,
thing would have been achieved; he would still have to
gotiate the courtyards; and after the courtyards the second,
rrounding palace; and steps and courtyards once again; and
t another palace; and so on for millennia; and if he finally fell
rough the outermost gate—but it can never, never happen—
e capital would lie before him, the middle of the world, its
egs piled high. No one gets through this, and certainly not
meone with a message from a dead man.—But you sit at
ur window and dream about it, as evening falls.

One of the octavo notebooks from the spring of 1917, with the
first manuscript of Report to an Academy

chönborn Palace

/hile Kafka was looking for a quiet study in the Little
uarter (Malá Strana) with his sister Ottla in the summer
16 (see p. 59), he was also wondering whether "there
ight be a quiet hole in some attic-room in one of the
d palaces, where I could finally stretch out in peace."

He found it a little later, in the **Schönborn Palace**
5] at 15 Marktgasse (Tržiště), an "apartment on the
cond floor, a rather lower room, a view of the garden,
ith windows facing on to the Hradčany." And:

ie garden! Passing through the gateway to the castle, you can
rdly believe what you see. Through the high arch of the sec-
d gateway flanked by caryatids one can see a beautifully
aced, double flight of stone steps leading slowly upward in a
oad sweep up to a gloriette.

arden side of the Schönborn Palace, Hradčany in the background

From March 1917, after giving up the apartment **At the Golden Pike** (see p. 57), Kafka lived in the **Schönborn Palace**, but he also continued to work in the little house in the **Alchimistengasse** (see p. 59), although no longer at night, because "it will be difficult to go out at night, as the gate cannot be unlocked from outside, but instead I can take a nice little stroll in a part of the park that is reserved for the royal family."

In the stories that Kafka wrote in the spring and summer of 1917, therefore, we cannot be sure which were written in the Alchimistengasse and which in the Schönborn Palace.

It was in the Schönborn Palace, in the night of August 12-13, that Kafka suffered his first "hemorrhage," heralding the pulmonary tuberculosis from which he died seven years later. "What happened was that the brain could no longer bear the cares and pains placed upon it. It said: 'I'm giving it up; but if there is still someone concerned with the preservation of the whole, then let him take some of my burden, and things will be all right for a while,'" Kafka later wrote to Milena. In September 1917 Kafka gave up the apartment and the study; he was embarking upon a series of stays in the country and sanatoria. When he returned to Prague (often to work in the office again—he was pensioned off only five years later) he lived with his parents in the **Oppelthaus** (see next page).

The Schönborn Palace is now home to the United States Embassy. Kafka's apartment was behind the three windows in the second story on the left. You can follow his walk home from the Alchimistengasse to the Schönborn Palace: through the castle and down the New Castle Steps (Zámecké schody) into the Nerudagasse (Nerudova), through the gateway of No. 13 Nerudagasse straight to the Schönborn Palace.

Oppelthaus, the Grave

fter his illness and his return from a first stay in the ountry, Kafka once again lived with his parents, from May to October 1918, in the **Oppelthaus** [21] (see . 48). Interrupted by his increasingly numerous visits to natoria, he had to do a great deal of work in the office, nd was in Prague from April to October 1919, from December 1919 to March 1920, from July to November 920, from September 1921 to January 1922. During lese periods, in the autumn of 1920 alone (in a room on le third story on the left of the staircase, with a view of le Altstädter Ring), he wrote a great deal, including "The City Coat of Arms," "Poseidon," "At Night," "On le Question of the Laws."

"Once when we were looking down from the win-ow to the Ring," Kafka's Hebrew teacher wrote at this me, "he said, pointing to the buildings: 'There was my ;ymnasium, in that building that overlooks the university nd a bit farther to the left my office. Within this little ircle'—and he drew a few little circles—'my whole life contained.'"

he St. Nicholas Market on the Altstädter Ring, around 1900

After a short convalescent holiday, in the course of which Kafka had started work on the manuscript of the novel *The Castle*, he lived in the Oppelthaus once again from the end of February to the end of June 1922. During these four months he produced chapters 6 to 1 of *The Castle*, and the short stories "First Sorrow" and "A Hunger Artist."

Kafka then returned to spend a considerable period of time living with his parents in Prague, from September 1922 to June 1923. In March 1924 he came back for a few weeks (during this period he wrote his last short story, "Josephine the Singer"; he died on June 3, 1924, in a sanatorium, and was buried in the Jewish Cemetery in Prague, in Straschnitz.

Kafka's **grave** is reached by underground line A Želivského Station. The short walk to the Jewish Cemetery (Židovské Hřbitovy; closed Friday afternoon and Saturday) is signposted, as is the walk to Kafka's grave (which has become a strange cult destination, with poems, petitions, and other votive offerings).

In tiefstem Schmerz geben wir bekannt, daß unser Sohn

JUDr. Franz Kafka

am 3. Juni im Sanatorium Kierling bei Wien, 41 Jahre alt, gestorben ist. Das Begräbnis findet am Mittwoch, den 11. Juni um $^3/_4$4 Uhr auf dem jüdischen Friedhof in Straschnitz statt.

PRAG, am 10. Juni 1924.

Hermann und **Julie Kafka,**
Eltern,
im Namen der trauernden Hinterbliebenen.

3892

Von Kondolenzbesuchen bitten wir abzusehen.

The Official's Career Path

Kafka as a clerk, about thirty-two, 1915-16

had started with his first walk to school, from the house **Minuta** (see p. 32), hand in hand with the cook. Kafka described it decades later; we can follow him and remember all his fears about school:

was our cook, a small, haggard, pointy-nosed woman, hollow-cheeked, yellowish, but solid, energetic, and superior, led me to school every morning. We lived in the house that separates the Kleine Ring from the Große Ring. So our path took first over the Ring, then into the Teingasse, then through a kind of arched gate into the Fleischmarktgasse and down to the Fleischmarkt. And now the same thing was repeated every morning for about a year. Upon leaving the house the cook said she would tell the teacher how naughty I had been at home. Well, I probably wasn't very naughty, but I was difficult, useless, sad, and angry, and something fine could probably always have been cobbled together for the teacher. I knew this, and so I did not take the cook's threat lightly. But at first I thought that the journey to school was terribly long, that a lot could happen in the meantime (it is from such apparent childish foolishness, because the journeys are not terribly long, that that anxiety and dead-eyed earnestness gradually develop) and I was also, at least while we were still in the Altstädter Ring, very dubious about whether the cook, who was a figure of authority, albeit only a domestic one, would dare to talk to the figure of authority-in-the-world that the teacher was.

Around the entrance to Fleischmarktgasse . . . fear of the threat gained the upper hand. . . . I began to plead, she shook her head, the more I begged, the more valuable what I was begging for seemed to me, and the greater the danger, I stopped and begged for forgiveness, she pulled me on, I threatened her with retaliation from my parents, she laughed, *here* she was omnipotent, I clung to the portals of the shops, to the cornerstones, I didn't want to go on before she had forgiven me, I pulled her back by her skirt (and it wasn't easy for her) but she dragged me on, it grew late, the Jakobskirche struck 8, we could hear the school bells, other children began to run, I was always most afraid of being late, now we had to run as well, and the consideration persisted: "She will say it, she won't say it"—well, she didn't say it, ever, but she always had the opportunity and even an apparently growing possibility (yesterday I didn't say it, but I will definitely say it today), and she never let go of that.

This is the walk described: from the Altstädter Ring (Staroměstké náměstí) to the Teingasse (Týnská) near the Teyn Church, then left into the Kleine Stupartsgasse (Malá Štupartská) and right into Fleischmarktgasse (Masná), at the other end of which is the Volksschule.

The elementary school on the Fleischmarkt

Volksschule

The **Deutsche Knabenvolksschule in Prag-Altstadt** [4] (16 Fleischmarktgasse / Masná), which Kafka attended from 1889 to 1893, was at the time a relatively new building on the meat market (although it did not have a playground; during recess the pupils stayed in their class rooms). A classmate of Kafka's writes: "We walked past the hanging pieces of meat, and on the left, opposite the butchers' shops, we passed a Czech Volksschule, at the entrance of which there was a quotation from Comenius 'A Czech child belongs in a Czech school,' and then on the right there was our school." During those years the battle between the nationalities even extended to children; fights between Czech and German pupils were commonplace.

The German Volksschule is now an apartment building, the Czech one is still in operation (11-13 Masná).

*The Gymnasium pupil,
about thirteen years old*

Gymnasium

he **Staats-Gymnasium mit deutscher Unter-
chtssprache in Prag-Altstadt** (German Gymnasium)
] was based in the rear building of the Kinsky Palais in
e Altstädter Ring (Staroměstské náměstí), the right-
nd front wing of which later also housed his father's
op as well (see p. 41).

Kafka attended this from September 1893 until his
hool-leaving examination in September 1901, always
arful

at I would not pass the end-of-year examinations, and if I
d, that I would not make any progress in the next class, and,
I were to avoid that through deception, that I would fail
finitively in my graduation examination and that I would
ite certainly, regardless of the precise moment, suddenly
veal some unimagined inability, and surprise my parents and
eryone else as well, lulled as they had been by my outwardly
gular progress.

A real anxiety, although we may take his assertion of a "unimagined inability" with a pinch of salt.

The Gymnasium is reached through the lefthand gateway of the front building, but the rear courtyard is no longer accessible.

Altstädter ring, 1896.
On the right the Kinsky Palace with the pupils' entrance
In the third house on the left, with the Hotel Goldhammer,
was his father's first shop.

fter the division of the University (1882), the law fac-
lty was given the **Karolinum** [8]; the German students
ntered the building via 11 Eisengasse (Železná), the
Czechs through the entrance at 3 Obstmarkt (Ovocný
h). From 1901 to 1906 Kafka also attended the **Juris-
rudence Seminar** at 5 Obstmarkt and in the **Political
cience Seminar** in the Clam-Gallas Palace, 20
lusgasse (Husova).

*he Karlinum, seen from the Eigengasse
ehind them the front colonnade of the Deutsche Landestheater*

It was here, then, that he heard lectures on Pandec
and Forensic Medicine, Financial Science and Ec
nomics, Statistics and Political Science, Personal La
Trade Law, International Law, and Legal History.

But he also visited the Deutsche Landstheater ne:
to the Karolinum, other theaters, cinemas, and cafés (s
p. 109), the debating circle in the **Café Louvre** (at 2
Ferdinandstrasse/Národní, on the first floor), or the le
ture evenings at the home of the chemist's wife Bertl

As a student in his "wine tavern period"

anta in the house **At the Unicorn** (17 Altstädter
ing/Staroměstské náměstí; in good condition, with the
eraldic beast on the front facade, see p. 25). And he reg-
arly attended the events of the liberal (as opposed to the
erman nationalist "Germania") students' association
eading and Debating Group of German Students
Prague, whose "literary correspondent" he was for a
me, and whose rooms were originally at 12
erdinandstrasse (Národní) (the building no longer
ists), and from 1904 at 14 Krakauergasse (Krakovská).

On June 16, 1906, Franz Kafka, at the age of just
venty-three, graduated as a Doctor of Law in the Hall
f the Karolinum.

oday, the Karolinum is still a university and easy to visit,
one is more or less student age, or if one has a digni-
ed, professorial air.

iew of the rooms of the Reading and Lecture Hall in the Krakauergasse

FRANZ KAFKA BEEHRT SICH ANZUZEIGEN, DASS
ER AM MONTAG DEN 18. JUNI D. J. AN DER K. K.
DEUTSCHEN KARL FERDINANDS-UNIVERSITÄT IN
PRAG ZUM DOKTOR DER RECHTE PROMOVIERT WURDE.

PRAG, IM JULI 1906.

*Franz Kafka is honored to learn that on Monday, June 18 of this
year, at the Imperial German Karl Ferdinands-Universität in Prague,
he graduated as Doctor of Law. Prague, July 1906.*

The *Gerichtsjahr*

By the time of his last graduation exam, Kafka w
already working for a lawyer (Dr. Richard Löwy, 1
Altstädter Ring/Staroměstské náměstí) for a few montl
in the summer of 1906, so that he could, in Octobe
1906, begin the *Gerichtsjahr* that was compulsory fo
law students who wanted to enter civil practice: si
months of civil court (October 1906 to March 1907
six months of criminal law (April to September 1907
Budding lawyers generally helped the judges by studyin
records and hearings.

The **Landeszivilgericht** (Higher District Civ
Court) [9] was in an old building with a beautifi
baroque doorway at 14 Obstmarkt (Ovocný trh) on th
corner with 36 Zeltnergasse (Celetná).

The **Landesstrafgericht** (Higher District Crimin.
Court) [10] was near the New Town Hall on the nort
side of Charles Square (Karlovo náměstí), on the corne
of Wassergasse (Vodičkova); later, Kafka would continu
to walk to Charles Square.

Both buildings are still standing.

Assicurazioni Generali

Kafka worked in the building of the insurance company **Assicurazioni Generali** [12], built around 1900 in the "Prague Baroque style" on Wenceslas Square (Václavské náměstí), on the corner of Heinrichsgasse (Jindřišská) at No. 29, from October 1907 to the middle of July 1908.

Before he could take up this post he had to undergo a medical examination ("height 1.82 m, weight 61 kg, slim, younger appearance"), and was taken on as a "temporary worker," "with a tiny income of 80 crowns," and the hope "that he might one day sit on the chairs of very distant lands."

Hopes swiftly dashed: Kafka later considered this period "particularly dreadful . . . with office hours from 8 in the morning until 7 in the evening, until 8:30. . . ." Only a few months later he was in search of alternative employment.

The Prague Baroque of the grandiose office building can still be admired, with its stucco vases and allegorical figures.

*The Assicurazioni Generali building
(on a postcard from Kafka to Max Brod, October 1910)*

77

Handels–Akademie (Business School)

In order to escape his unloved job with **Assicurazion** **Generali** (see previous page), from February to Ma 1908 Kafka attended evening classes, a "course in work ers' insurance" at the **Prager Handels-Akademie** [13 at 8 Fleischmarktgasse (Masná), clearly as a preparatio for his planned application to the **Arbeiter-Unfall Versicherungs-Anstalt** (Workers' Accident Insuranc Institute) (see next page). Three officials with th Workers' Accident Insurance Institute who taught at th Handels-Akademie would later become Kafka's superior or colleagues.

The school occupied the upper two stories of th three-story building (still standing).

The Business Academy on the Fleischmarkt

Workers' Accident Insurance Institute

Kafka first entered the building of the **Arbeiter-Unfall-Versicherungs-Anstalt für das Königreich Böhmen in Prag** (Workers' Accident Insurance Institute for the Kingdom of Bohemia in Prague) [14] at 7 Poříč, built in 1896, on July 30, 1908. At eight o'clock in the morning, as he would then do every day, give or take a few minutes, dashing up the stairs to the fourth floor. Officially the office closed at 2 PM, but usually rather later. Taken on as "temporary staff," he was made "Concipist"—or articled clerk—in 1910, vice secretary 1913, secretary in 1920, secretary in chief in 1922; on July 1, 1922, Kafka was retired.

Workers' accident insurance was introduced in Austria in 1889, and organized on a regional basis. The insurance institute in Prague, responsible for the kingdom of Bohemia, was by far the largest in the monarchy. Suffering a deficit for the first twenty years, it was reorganized in 1907, and with the "payroll obligation" decreed in 1909, the institute could finally afford to seek out and act against the evasions constantly practiced by businesses. By 1910 it was in a position to present a positive balance sheet, although the number of accidents was still on the rise for the time being (in 1912, out of 573,240 parties insured, there were 9,753 accidents).

Initially, Kafka's work involved classifying businesses according to their "risk quotient," and organizing inspections; later he drew up the appeals against the companies' objections, represented the institute in the court (actions against contribution evasion, enforcement of compensation claims), and dealt with accident protection (see the text below from 1910).

In Kafka's day, the Prague Workers' Accident Insurance Institute was very large, with over 250 clerks, and seventy clerks worked in his division, the "companies division," covering classification, contributions, inspections. Kafka was one of the representatives of the division manager, and one of the three (token) Jews in the institute, which was managed almost exclusively by German officials, while the overwhelming majority of the other clerks spoke Czech.

Kafka's superiors considered his work outstanding; he was popular in the institute, and had no enemies. But over the years the fate of the workers depressed him ("How modest these people are, they come to us with their requests. Instead of storming the institute and smashing everything to bits"), and the office struck him as more and more "horrific" because it held back his literary work "for the sake of some wretched file or other."

The institute's building, which now houses an electronic assembly company, is in good condition, with long, labyrinthine passageways, a front and a rear staircase, a courtyard, two entrances (with coats of arms: on the left the imperial two-headed eagle, on the right the Bohemian lion), the righthand entrance having a porter's lodge with which Kafka was already familiar. For the first few years Kafka's room was on the fourth floor, and later (probably from 1913) on the first floor; we do not know whether it was in the middle room with the balcony or in the room on the outside right. If you wish to do so you can stay in the adjoining hotel (which stood there in Kafka's day; then it was the Angleterre, today the Atlantic) and put your ear to the wall.

Prague office, 1907

*The Workers' Accident Insurance Institute, 1914
Top right, the company seal. On the left, in the neighboring
building, the entrance to the "Bio-Elite" movie theater (see p. 118)*

Franz Kafka, *Accident Prevention Regulations in the Use of Wood-Planing Machines*

Our illustrations show the difference between square shafts and round shafts from the point of view of protection technique. The blades of the square shaft (Ill. 1), fastened directly to the shaft with screws, rotate with a bare blade at a rate of 3,800–4,000 rotations per minute. The risks to the worker that arise as a result from the great distance between the blade-shaft and the table surface are clearly apparent. Thus people have either worked with these shafts in ignorance of the danger, which may thus have become even greater, or else they have worked with an awareness of constant and inevitable danger. An extremely careful worker might take care to ensure that while working, that is, while passing the piece of wood over the knife of the plane, no joint of the finger protruded over the tool, but the chief risk defied any amount of caution. Even the hand of the most cautious worker would slip into the blade-gap if he should slip, or if, as happened on not infrequent occasions, the wood sprang back when he pressed the piece that was to be planed on the work surface with one hand and guided it toward the plane-shaft with the other.

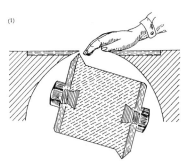

(1)

It was possible neither to predict nor to prevent the wood rising up and springing back, for this happened if the wood was deformed or knotty in certain places, if the blades did not revolve quickly enough or were in poor condition, or if the pressure of the hands on the wood was unevenly distributed. But an accident such as this could not occur without the loss of several finger-joints, or even whole fingers. (Ill. 2)

This square shaft is, in Ills. 3 and 4, compared with a safety shaft in the engineering factory of Bohumil Voleský, Prague-Lieben, and in Ills. 5 and 6 with an original safety shaft for

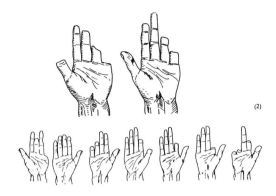

wood-planing machines following the Schrader System, a product of the engineering factory Emil Mau and Co. in Dresden.

The blades of this shaft are embedded, completely protected, between the flap (Voleský shaft) or a wedge (Patent Schrader) and the massive body of the shaft. They are fixed and

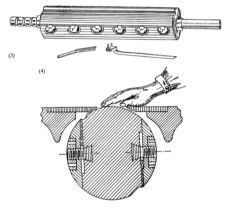

free of external influences, and it is just as impossible for the blades to leap out as it is for them to buckle or bend. It is equally impossible for the screws to fly out in the event of a breakdown, as the screws are round, lie deep in depressions in the flaps, and also, in the Schrader Patent, are less taxed than the screws in the square shafts, since in these the screws have to hold the knives themselves, while in the round shaft the screws have only to hold the flaps against the wedges, which is all the easier since these flaps are only fixed at their outer extremities,

while also being separated by a gap from the body of the sha
in a way that cannot be seen in the illustration

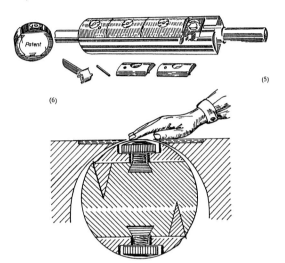

(5)

(6)

But the most important thing as regards protection technniqu
is that only the edges of the knives protrude, and that thes
knives, since they practically grow into the shaft, and can b
quite thin, without the risk of breaking.

The introduction of these devices removes the predominan
possibility of catching one's fingers in the gap of the square
shaft plane, but even if the fingers do enter the gap, it ensure
that only quite insignificant injuries can arise, minor cuts th
do not even lead to an interruption of the work.

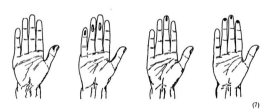

(7)

Favorite Walks

In Karlsgasse, 1900

Kafka was a great walker and *flâneur*, on holidays, in the evening, even at night, for hours, often alone. This clearly had much to do with his writing technique. Hardly any notes or sketches, but lengthy mental preparation, "the monstrous world that I have in my head," which he then usually wrote down "in one go": "It's the only way to write," he noted in his diary after his first experience with "The Judgment." And: "The strength that I derive from the least bit of writing is unquestionable and wonderful. The look with which I surveyed everything on my walk yesterday!"

Here are three of the walks of which Kafka was particularly fond.

With his sister Ottla, in front of the Oppelthaus, 1814

1. On the Laurenziberg

Kafka visited Prague's local hill, the **Laurenziberg** (Petřín), as a schoolboy; his earliest surviving narrative fragment, *Description of a Struggle*, deals with a nighttime walk in winter through the city and up the Laurenziberg. In the very first pages we find ourselves at the Charles Bridge, at **Kreuzherrenplatz** [A] (Křižovnické náměstí), with the monument to Charles IV, the founder of the first German university, erected in 1848. Four faculties stand at his feet, with Jurisprudence on the right. It is here, then, that the law student Franz Kafka stands (1904) and has his surreal hero say:

I swayed and had to look firmly at the statue of Charles IV to be sure of my position. But the moonlight was clumsy and set Charles IV in motion. I was astonished, and my feet grew much

88

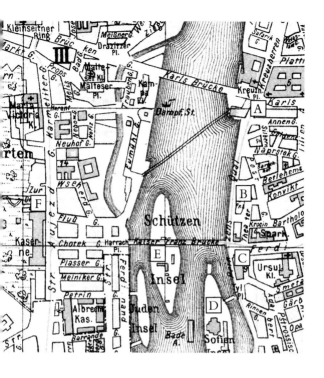

more powerful, for fear that Charles IV might fall over if I did not adopt a calming posture. Later my effort struck me as futile, because Charles IV fell over anyway. . . . But lest anyone later tell me that anyone can swim over the pavement and it is not worth telling about, I hauled myself over the railings with a spring, and, swimming, circled each of the statues of the saints. . . .

Let us leave the young man flying around the statues of the Charles Bridge, and turn upriver into the Franzensquai (today: Smetanovo nábřeží), in the middle of which stands the **Kaiser Franz Monument** [B]: at the top is the emperor, with all manner of allegories beneath. In 1918 the emperor was removed, and his place was left empty. A note of Kafka's from 1920 clearly refers to this:

It was an early part of a monumental group. Around some kind of raised center, in a precisely calculated figuration, stood symbols of the soldiery, the arts, the sciences, craftsmen. The group has been broken up long since, or at least he has left it and carries himself alone through his life.

Cross Ferdinandstrasse (Národní), go past the Czech **National Theater** [C] (which Kafka, unlike most Prague Germans, did not shun) into the Riegerquai (today: Masarykovo nábřeží), with its beautiful art nouveau houses. On the right a little bridge (on which there was also a toll to pay) led to the Sofieninsel [D] (today Slovanský ostrov).

Kafka often visited the Sofieninsel, a "place often visited by Czech high society" with a beautiful park restaurant, ballrooms, and lecture halls (Kafka heard Hofmannsthal there), warm water baths and a "swimming school" in the Moldau. It was here, too, that—as he delighted in telling his friend Milena in 1920— the swimming teacher asked the thirty-seven-year-old institute secretary Dr. Kafka whether he could row building contractor over the Moldau, mistaking him for a boy whom he wanted to "give the pleasure of a free boat journey," and also the owner of the swimming school, "big Trnka, came along and asked whether the boy could swim." The "boy" accepted, but sadly did not receive a tip, and immediately rowed back, more "swollen with pride" than he had been for a long time.

Return to the Riegerquai and cross the Kaiser Franz Brücke (today: most Legií), in the middle of which flight of steps branches down toward **Schützen Island** [E] (Střelecký ostrov), with a park in the northern part, an inn and rifle range in the southern part, a meeting place for the Prague Germans.

The street continues straight to the Aujezdgasse (Újezd) on the right, the first little alley on the left (U lanové dráhy) leads to the valley station [F] of the Laurenziberg funicular railway, installed in 1891. Before you lies a gently rising meadow, some of it terraced, with

he Kaiser-Franz-Brücke shortly after its opening in 1901.
the middle, the Schützeninsel, in the background the
aurenziberg with the Observation Tower

)n the Schützeninsel: the rifle club lining up in orderly fashion
r the photographer, around 1890

View from the Laurenziberg, around 1890, with the Kaiser-Franz-Brücke over the Schützeninsel. In the background the Nationaltheater and (on the right) the Sophieninsel (Žofín) In the right-hand foreground, the Hunger Wall

View from the Castle approach toward the Hohler Weg and Strahov Monastery, about 1918

ge numbers of trees (including many fruit trees): the **minargarten** [G] (Seminářská zahrada). On the left, e "Hunger Wall," built in 1360, which inspired Kafka's ort story "The Great Wall of China."

Three years later, in 1920, he remembered an experi-ce that he had had as a student, or even as a schoolboy, the slope of the Laurenziberg, which had determined aesthetic from that point onward:

ie day many years ago I was sitting, doubtless sad enough, on slope of the Laurenziberg. I was examining the wishes that ad for my life. The most important or charming was the sh to achieve a view of life (and—this was necessarily bound with it—to convince other people of it in writing), in ich life maintained its natural heavy rise and fall, but at the ne time would be recognized, no less clearly, as a void, a am, a floating. A fine wish, perhaps, if I had wished it prop-y. As a wish, say, to hammer together a table with painstak-ly ordered craftness and at the same time to do nothing, not that one might say: "Hammering is nothing to him," but or him hammering is real hammering and at the same time thing at all," whereby the hammering would become even lder, even more resolute, even more real and, if you like, even re insane.

But he could not wish like this, for his wish was not a wish, was only a defense, an embourgeoisement of nothing, a ath of merriment that he wanted to give to nothing, which was barely making his first conscious steps into at that e, but which he already felt to be his element. It was at time a kind of farewell that he took from the illusory world youth, it had never directly deluded him, incidentally, but ly allowed him to be deluded by the speeches of all the horities around him.

you have already taken your farewell from youth and traveling by funicular railway: get out at the middle p, at the Hasenburg Restaurant [H] (Nebozízek), ich was already popular in Kafka's day, and walk to the of the Laurenziberg with the Observation Tower [I] m the top of which you can see many of Kafka's walks d the places where he worked and lived.

View from the Seminary Garden (Seminářska zahrada)
to the Charles Bridge (middle) and the Teyn Church.
On the left the gloriette in the park of the Schönborn Palace

r your return journey via the Hradčany you now have
o possibilities.

ther stay on the path at the top of the slope [J], walk-
g along the Hunger Wall and looking back through the
od on the left: Here, barely recognizable, were the
ahov quarries [K] (now the Strahov stadium), the place
which Josef K. is brought in the closing chapter of *The
ial*, "a small quarry, abandoned and barren. . . ."

n the right is Strahov Monastery [L] whose literary
hive contains the personal files of Kafka the insurance
n. The Hohle Weg (Úvoz) and Nerudagasse
erudova) will then bring you back to the Charles
idge.

:: Come back along the Ewige Stiege [M] (Petřinské
ody), which joins the Wälsche Gasse (Vlaška), past
Schönborn Palace (see p. 63) to the Marktgasse
žiště) to the Charles Bridge.

Nerudagasse: the first automobile in Prague, 1898

2. Across the Belvedere to Chotek Park and the Little Quarter

This walk leads past what Kafka considered the "m[ost] beautiful place" in Prague. You can start at the house [of] **the Ship** [A] (see p. 42), now the Hotel Intercontinent[al,] where "The Judgment" was written, with a view [of] the balustrade of the Čech Bridge (Niklasbrücke), fr[om] which Georg Bendemann hangs himself.

Either walk past him politely and cross the brid[ge,] climbing up to the **Crown Prince Rudolf Park** [B] (now: Letná Park), which was generally known, to Ka[fka] as well, as the **Belvedere** (not to be confused with t[he] Belvedere Castle; see below) on a new flight of st[eps] leading to a plateau on which, for a fairly short period [of] time, there once stood an enormous statue of Stalin.

Or leave Georg Bendemann, and hence literature,
anging there, and turn right down stream over the
antišek [C] to the Elizabeth or Franz Josef Bridge (now
ermův most). Cross the bridge and then turn either left
right out of the tunnel into the Belvedere Park. There
ed to be a coffeehouse and a restaurant here (there
as been another one on the right at the top since the
xties, called Expo 58, with a beautiful view) and, most
mportantly, a fine funicular railway [D], which brought
sitors to the plateau. At the top of the Belvedere, walk
ward Hradčany, past the tennis courts to the extremely
gly "Stalin plateau."

Top: View from the Hanavský Pavilion, 1911
On the left the Čech Bridge, with the house At the Ship.
On the right the Chain Bridge, with the foundations of the
new Mánes Bridge. Behind it, the Charles Bridge

Bottom: The Hanavský Pavilion at its opening in the Belvedere

o on through the Belvedere Park to the beautifully
stored Hanavský Pavilion, which is still a café, with a
eautiful view from the balustrade:

On the left is the Čech Bridge, and just next it the
uilding of the **Civilian Swimming School** [F] (see
44), straight ahead are more recent university buildings,
ext to them on the right the **Rudolfinum** [O] (see
114), formerly approached by an iron pedestrian bridge
to the Chotek Park. This is a new bridge. Formerly the
udolfinum was reached by a pedestrian bridge (the
"Kettensteg"), which was replaced in 1912 by what is
ow the Mánes Bridge [N] (Mánesúv most). Farther
ack on the right are the Charles Bridge and the
ational Theater. To the right below the balustrade is the
rakasche Akademie, in front of which is the former site
' the Military Swimming School.

From the Hanavský Pavilion, continue walking
rough the Belvedere Park toward Gogolstrasse
Gogolova); on the left a small footbridge leads to
hotek Park. The bridge is new; formerly one crossed
e (now very busy) Chotekstrasse (Chotkova) and
tered the park through a gate.

In the Belvedere

Chotek Park with Belvedere Palace

…afka considered **Chotek Park** [G] "the most beautiful …ace in Prague. Birds sang, the castle with its gallery, …e old trees hung with early leaves, the half-light." This …astle with its gallery" is the famous "Italian" **Belvedere …alace** [H] (1538-63), with the "Singing Fountain" …ove it in the Königsgarten (Královská zahrada).

Walk past the Königsgarten along the Marienschanze …Mariánské hradby), from which the "midday salute"used … be fired. At the end of the Marienschanze, turn left …to the street leading to the Palace courtyard, across …e Hirschgraben [I] (Jelení Příkop), which Kafka was …le to look down upon from his little house in the …lchimistengasse (see p. 59).

You can (keeping to the left) visit him there, taking in …visit to the Choir of St.Vitus' Cathedral in honor of the …thedral chapter of *The Trial*, and then return to the city …a the Alte Schloßstiege (see p. 60).

…therwise, you can bear right and pass through the …oyal Palace, taking a look at the palace guard ("In the …iddle of the first palace courtyard I stood and watched … palace guard alert") and arrive, via the Neue …hloßstiege, at the **Kleinseitner Ring** (Malostranské …ámĕstí), the former center of political power, with what …afka called the "Zionsburg," the Statthalterei or …overnor's Building [J], the Bohemian parliament [K], …e General (or Corps) Commando [L], the Ober- …ndesgericht (provincial appeal court) [M] and a large …triotic Radetzky monument, which was torn down in …e first year of the new Czechoslovak republic.

Of course, Kafka did not only come here on walks …ooking at the fountain in the Palais Thun or visiting …e Radetzky Café with his blind friend Oskar Baum; …e p. 121), he also came on official business, both … the Appeal Court and in the Statthalterei, as a legal …presentative of the Workers' Accident Insurance …stitute.

Return to Josefstadt via the Belvederegasse (Letensk. and the Mánes Bridge [N], which replaced the "Ketten steg," continue along the Salnitergasse (now 17 listopadu with (on the left) the **Rudolfinum** [O] and (on th right) the **Craft Museum** [P], where Kafka liked to us the reading room (see pp. 114 and 116).

Or take the route from the Kleinseitner Ring over th Charles Bridge, back into the Altstadt.

Kafka once jotted down a shortened form of this walk i his diary: "By chance I took the opposite journey from my usual one, Kettensteg, Hradčany, Charles Bridge Usually this journey just brings me down, today, comin from the opposite direction, I have elevated myself some what."

Chain Bridge with the Rudolfinum (left)

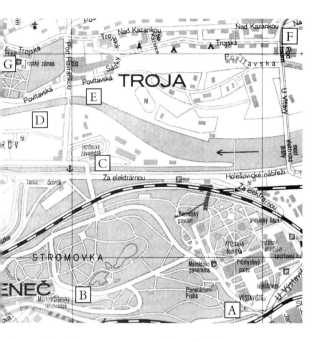

. Into the Baumgarten and to Troja

Let us go to the Baumgarten . . . there is music there
. . there is shouting and hurdy-gurdies are playing in the
venues. . . ." If you wish to follow this suggestion from
he hero of Kafka's *Description of a Struggle* and make what
still a favorite outing for the people of Prague, do what
iey did then, and still do: Take the tram, which was
orse-drawn in those days, but was later electrified, as it
today. The best one to take is from Josefsplatz (náměstí
Republiky), line No. 5 to the entrance [A].

To the right of the entrance are beautifully restored
uildings dating from the time of the first Bohemian
ibilee Exhibition (1891) and later on. To the left is the
ctual **Baumgarten** (Stromovka), in which "each after-
oon, once the weather permits light music in the open,
rague's high society meets in the well-appointed café
3]. With shady avenues, beautiful meadows, fountains,
id flower beds. More than a hundred different species of

tree are identified by Latin, Czech, and German name on little panels."

Kafka spent a great deal of time here, "in the restaurant," "by the pool, listening to the music," with his sister Ottla, with friends and acquaintances. But he also often walked on, through the Baumgarten over the little can bridge [C] to the **Kaiserinsel** [D] (Císařský ostrov). you wish to follow the same route, follow the signpost for the Zoo (Zoologická zahrada).

The institute secretary liked to lie in the grass: "I w lying there recently when a rather elegant man wit whom I sometimes have official dealings drove past in carriage and pair. I stretched out and felt the joy (although only the joys) of being *déclassé*." He found place like this on the Kaiserinsel as well:

Near here, behind the Baumgarten on a high embankmen there is a little wood at the edge of which I like to lie. On th left you can see the river, and beyond it thinly wooded peak opposite me an isolated hill with an old house that has struc me as mysterious since I was a child, softly embedded in i surroundings, and all around peaceful, undulating countrysid

It seems that this may have been a spot on the road th crosses the Kaiserinsel, and which until 1984 was linke by a ferry (now a pedestrian bridge) with the Troja palac and estate.

While Kafka is being ferried [the text has "translated but I'm not sure the joke works.—Trans.] across the rive cross the pedestrian bridge and join up with him aga on the other side, in September with his sister Ottla:

We were in two wonderful places that I have also recently di covered, again near Troja but even more beautiful than the edg of that wood. One place in the grass, still deep, but surroun ed all around, at various distances, by low embankments, an quite exposed to the blissful sun. The other is not far off, a dee narrow, varied valley. Both places as quiet as paradise once th people have been driven away. To disturb the peace I read Pla to Ottla, and she is teaching me to sing. I must have go somewhere in my throat, even if it wishes only to sound lik tin.

Horse-drawn tram to the Baumgarten, 1890

*Electric tram to the Baumgarten, on the Franz-Josef-Brücke,
c. 1910*

The Pomological Institute in Troja, ca. 1900-1905

In 1918 Kafka regularly went to Troja, to garden in the Pomological Institute. The city dweller had always been fascinated by gardening. In 1913 he had worked for a gardener in Nusle (19 Slupergasse/Na slupi), and from autumn 1917 to 1918 he had helped his sister Ottla on her "little garden" in Zürau (northwest Bohemia).

The **Institute of Pomology, Wine-Growing, and Gardening** had been founded some time previously by an "imperial patriotic and economic society in the kingdom of Bohemia," as a "place of training for those who wish to prepare themselves for practical gardening." This is exactly what Kafka wanted (as preparation for a planned journey to Palestine, among other things), and also tried to persuade his friend Max Brod, who collected him from there a number of times, of the advantages of working on the land.

Happily, although it is somewhat dilapidated, the building of the Pomological Institute still stands, on the corner of Trojská/Pod lisem [F].

You can either travel back with bus No. 112 (to Holešovice station, and continue on the underground, or go on to visit the **Troja Palace** [G] and the Zoo opposite, and return to Prague on the same bus or a boat from below the Troja Palace.

Literary Places and Entertainments

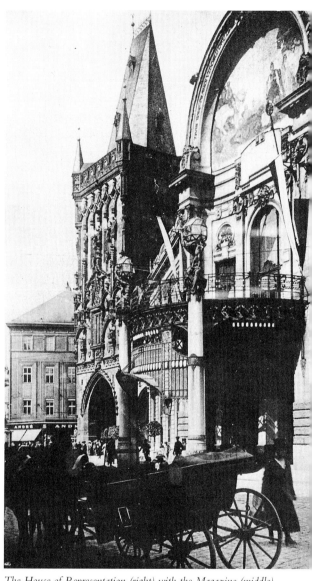

The House of Representation (right) with the Magazine (middle)
On the left behind the corner house zum Graben (Na Příkopě) with the
Buchhaltung André (ca. 1915)

afka visited the theater and attended lectures occasionally, he could be an ardent film-goer, he was a keen user f libraries (and kept a sharp eye on bookshop displays), ent whole nights in taverns as a student, later sometimes visited cafés and—as an excellent swimmer and arsman—enjoyed going on outings. On only one occason did he read from his own works in his home town.

elow are some venues that are still standing.

heaters, Lecture Halls

afka seldom went to the **Deutsche Landestheater** ee pp. 74 and 118), and attended the Czech **Nationaleater** (see p. 90) rather more often. Much more equently he visited Angelo Neumann's important **Neue Deutsche Theater** (now: Smetanovo divadlo) in ie City Park (Wilsonova 8).

It was here, for example, that he saw Schnitzler's *)as weite Land*, Hauptmann's *Der Biberpelz*, Wedekind's *rdgeist* (with the author in the title role), Max allenberg, and Albert Bassermann.

he Neue Deutsche Theater, ca. 1900

The Café Savoy on the Ziegenplatz

An jeden Sonn- und Feiertag auch Nachmittags-
vorstellung um ½4 Uhr.

Herrmanns Café-Restaurant „Savoy",

Prag, Ziegenplatz.   Regie S. Klug.

Original-jüdische Gesellschaft aus Lemberg.

Heute literarisch-dramatischer Abend.

Zum Schluß: 15864

Der wilde Mensch

von Gordon. Titelrolle: M. J. Löwy.

Anfang gegen 9 Uhr.   15805   Anfang gegen 9 Uhr.

Kafka's best-loved theater, between 1910 and 1912, however, was not really a theater, but a shabby café, **Café Savoy** [17] on the Ziegenplatz, on the corner of Ziegengasse and Stockhausgasse (Kozí/Vězeňská), where Yiddish theater troupe used to perform. It was there that Kafka saw thousands of performances of the most recent Yiddish plays—details of the contents of plays, remarks about actors or performances cover hundreds of pages of his diaries. One actor, Jizchak Löwy, became his friend; he told him, often two or three times a week, about Jewish life in Poland, and read him Yiddish poems.

The "café" has been preserved, is still a bar with (on the left) the taproom and (on the right) a small auditorium. The plays were performed in a corner of the auditorium, with a curtain hung diagonally.

The Jewish actor
Jizchak Löwy, 1913

The Jewish Town Hall, with the Altneusynagoge, 1905

Kafka delivered two lectures in the hall of the **Jewish Town Hall** [18] (Židovská radnice), 18 Maiselgasse (Maislova).

Once (1913), for a Jewish benevolent organization ("free cup of tea and cake") he read Kleist's *Michael Kohlhaas*, one of his favorite pieces of writing: "very small boys in the front row," filled with "innocent boredom."

Before this, on February 18, 1912, he introduced a reading by his friend Jizchak Löwy in the Jewish Town Hall (with the surviving text "Rede über die jiddische Sprache" (Speech on the Yiddish Tongue): "With delight and trust in Löwy and trust, proud, heavenly awareness during my lecture . . . , strong voice, effortless memory," he writes in his diary. Even Prague's Jewish weekly newspaper mentions "an elegant and charming lecture delivered by Dr. Kafka. . . ."

The lecture theater of the Jewish Town Hall is on the first floor on the right-hand side (four high windows).

In the **Hotel Erzherzog Stefan** [20] (now: Hotel Evropa) at 37 Wenzelsplatz (Václavské náměstí) (now No. 25) [NB text has 29, incorrectly.—Trans.], at the invitation of the recently founded "Johann Gottfried Herder Asociation for the promotion of theoretical interests," On December 4, 1912, Kafka read the story "The Judgment," written just four months previously. The audience was small, and it was really "only a private event." The critic Paul Wiegler, whose name was just becoming known, immediately wrote of the "arrival of a great, passionate and disciplined talent."

The present-day Hotel Evropa, an unusually beautifully preserved Art Nouveau building, is certainly worth seeing. The café is on two floors, and on the upper floor, behind the cast-iron-barred door, is the mirrored hall in which Kafka read.

The counter in the Hotel Erzherzog Stefan, 1905

The Rudolfinum
In the background on the left the Hanavský Pavilion
in the Belvedere, ca. 1910

In the **Rudolfinum**, mentioned above (at Jan-Palach Platz/Náměstí Jana Palacha, see p. 102), Kafka visited exhibitions of modern art, concerts (rarely) and lectures particularly one by Alexander Moissi: "Unnatural appearance. He sits apparently peacefully, sometimes with his hands folded between his knees, his eyes in the book lying open before him, and allows his voice to fall upon us with the breath of a running man."

In the **Municipal House** (Obecní dům) at No. Josefsplatz (náměstí Republiky [Please note spelling.– Trans.), a beautiful example of Prague's Art Nouveau style (see p. 108), built in 1910, Kafka heard a lecture by a Czech Social Democrat politician who was to have great influence on the novel *Der Verschollene [Amerika* František Soukup's account of his lecture tour of workers' associations in the United States.

Bookshops, Libraries

The three bookshops in which Kafka regularly found out about recent publications were, apart from the **André'sche Buchhandlung** at No. 39 Am Graben (Na příkopě) (see p. 108) and the **Neugebauersche Buchhandlung** at No. 20 Graben, particularly the **Calve'sche Hofbuchhandlung** at No. 12 Kleiner Ring (Malé náměstí), in the building At the Golden Lily. This building, with its coat of arms, has been beautifully restored.

The Kleine Ring with the Calve'sche Hofbuchhandlung (right)

Like his income, Kafka's library was not very large; so he was familiar with borrowing books. He used either the **Cassinelli lending library** or the nearby **University library** in the Clementinum, entry on Marienplatz (Márianské náměstí). The public reading room in the **Craft Museum** (see p. 102), in which Kafka often used to sit, has already been mentioned; and the "250 newspapers" of the **Café Continental** (see p. 120) held certain appeal.

The reading room in the Craft Museum

inema, Cabaret

he first traveling "living pictures" were shown in Prague
the turn of the century, in hotels, cafés, and department
ores. In the courtyard of the **Orient** café the first
ponymous) movie theater opened in October 1907.
afka visited it only a few months later, when it was
owing *The Thirsty Gendarme* and *The Gallant
uardsman*. Café and movie theater were at No. 20
ibernergasse (Hybernská), and the building was torn
wn (I was sadly a witness) in 1993.

From 1908 onward many new movie houses were
unded, originally in pub halls, like the Bio (as cinemas
ere called at the time) in U vejvodu (No. 2 Ägidi-
sse/Jilská).

e *"Bio u vejvodu"*

A little later saw the arrival of more elegant establishments such as the **Grand Théâtre Bio "Elite,"** right beside Kafka's office, in the surviving building No. 5 Pořič (see p. 81). Here Kafka saw *The White Slave, Alone at Last!*, and *The Disaster in the Dock*. A quite uninhibited consumer of short melodramatic pieces, he noted in his diary: "Was in the cinema. Cried. *Lolotte*. The good pastor. The little bicycle. The parents' reconciliation. Boundless entertainment."

The same was true of the "scientific-cinematographic presentations" in the **Deutsche Landestheater** (now Tyltheater, opposite the Karolinum), with films about strange insects (two months before the writing of "The Metamorphosis"!), the island of Ceylon, Danzig, or the life of Theodor Körner.

But the chief attraction for Kafka and his friend Max Brod was the revue theater **Lucerna** [16] (No. 4 Wassergasse/Vodičkova), whose "enormous building has rapidly turned into one of the most popular evening venues of pleasure-loving Prague." It was here that he saw the tragedian Mella Mars, the cabaret artist Fritz Grünbaum, and the music-hall singer Lucie König, noted the love scenes modeled on postcards, and clowns jumping over chairs into the wings. But also: "Behind us a man fell from his seat with boredom."

The Lucerna Palace is in good condition, and is still used as a cinema and place of entertainment.

Inside view of the auditorium of the Kabarett Lucerna

he wine bars with lovely names like Eldorado and rocadero (both on Obstmarkt/Ovocný trh), in which afka "spent many evenings sitting around," have sadly isappeared. Also gone are the **Café City** (No. 30 iklasstraße/Pařížká), in which Kafka often met Jizchak öwy (see p. 111), and the café **Corso** (No. 37 Am raben/Na příkopé) on the first floor, which Kafka and rod liked to visit early in their friendship: "In the ezession genre. Meeting place of the beauties from the illet, the Variété Chantant, and Prague's big business." he young men naturally wanted to watch, and were ust about able to afford this pleasure."

side of the Café Corso

Still in good condition (and still a café) is the Art Nouveau Café **Louvre** (see p. 74).

The **Café Continental** (No. 7 Am Graben/Na příkopě) was part of the Kolowrat palace, on the first floor, now occupied by—what else?—a bank. It was the largest café in Prague, with billiard rooms and gaming rooms, a venue frequented by German bourgeois society. Kafka visited it now and then, not only because of all its newspapers, but also to watch people playing cards.

The **Deutsche Haus** (No. 26 Am Graben/Na příkopě—now No. 22) in a baroque palace, was bought by the "German Casino" in 1873 and extended into a center—with nationalist tendencies—for Prague Germans (see also p. 12). Kafka was rarely a guest.

More often, on the other hand, he visited the **Café Arco** at No. 16 Hibernergasse (Hybernská), which soon became a meeting-point for the slightly younger writers in the circle around Franz Werfel (Paul Kornfeld, Egon Erwin Kisch, Otto Pick). Admittedly, Kafka had "mixed feelings amidst the young people. . . ."

The café, slightly altered but still with a billiard lounge, still exists: Kavárna Arco.

Inside of the Café Arco

The Radetzky Monument on the Kleinseitner Ring
On the left the Café Radetzky

One fine café that can still be visited, and one
which Kafka often stopped off on his walks, is the
Café Radetzky (today: Malostranská kavárna) at No. 30
Kleinseitner Ring (Malostranské náměstí). It got its name
from the Radetzky Monument which used to dominate
this "official" Prague square (see p. 101).

The two **Swimming schools** that Kafka particularly
loved, the one on the Sophieninsel (Žofín) (see p. 90) and
the Civilian Swimming School by the Čech Bridge (see
p. 40) have already been mentioned.

High society at the racing in Kuchelbad, 1909

Anyone wishing to recreate Kafka's **outings** should—recollecting *Thoughts for Gentlemen Horse Riders*—take look at the "Racecourse of the Prague Horse-Racin Society" in **Kuchelbad** (Chuchle), which is still in use

Or travel up or down the Vltava on one of Kafk much-loved pleasure boats.

Kafka's favorite journey, which he made on mar occasions, was to **Dobrichowitz** (Dobříchovice) on tl Berounka river.

spectfully yours, Dr. Franz Kafka

ources

he whole range of topographical and biographical research into
afka was used for this travel reader: some errors have been discreet-
corrected, and the results of more recent research incorporated. It
impossible to name all the sources here.

But now and again readers will want to know the source of a
afka quotation, in order to have a better understanding of their
ace in time or in literary or biographical context. These sources are
ted with reference to the 1950 ff. Fischer edition (the more easily
cessible, although this work also draws upon the *Kritische Ausgabe*
1982 ff.). The following references are used: B = *Beschreibung eines*
umpfes (Description of a Struggle) (1954), BP = *Beschreibung eines*
umpfes, Parallelausgabe, ed. Dietz (1969), Br = *Briefe* (Letters) (1958),
= *Erzählungen* (Stories) (1952), F = *Briefe an Felice* (Letters to
lice) (1967), H = *Hochzeitsvorbereitungen auf dem Lande* (Wedding
eparations in the Country) (1953), Mi = *Briefe an Milena* (Letters
Milena), *Neuausgabe* (1983), T = *Tagebuch* (Diary) (1951). Sources
llow the sequence in the text.

eface: Br 14, Br 101, T 367, H 131, F 571
fka's Prague: F 87, B 94
fka's Life: H 203, H 307, F 302, Br 109, F 67, Br 159
inuta: F 193, H 166, T 508, Mi 127
the Three Kings: F 79, F 109, Mi 196, E 43
e "shop": H 185
the Ship: F 120, Br 55, T 78, T 293, E 67, T 127
ax Brod's Apartment: T 285
opelthaus: F 480
lekgasse: T 420, T 418, T 421
rudagasse: F 618, T 438, T 440, T 449, T 454, F 626, T 456
the Golden Pike: F 630, F 632, F 631
chimistengasse: F 750, F 747, E 169
hönborn Palace: F 750, F 751, F 750, F 752, Mi 7
e Official's Career Path: Mi 71
mnasium: T 225
sicurazioni Generali: Br 48
orkers' Accident Insurance Institute: Max Brod, *Über Franz Kafka*
(1966) 76, T 77, Franz Kafka, *Amtliche Schriften* (1984) 134
vorite Walks: T 306, T 293, T 336
aurenziberg: BP 36, B 295, Mi 205, B 293
otek Park: T 467, T 182, T 358
umgarten: BP 138, T 539, F 558, F 674, F 677, F 693
eaters, Lecture Halls: T 341, T 251, F 162, T 263
nema, Cabaret: T 330, T 278
afés, Outings: F 228, Brod/Kafka, *Briefwechsel* (1989) 37, T 252

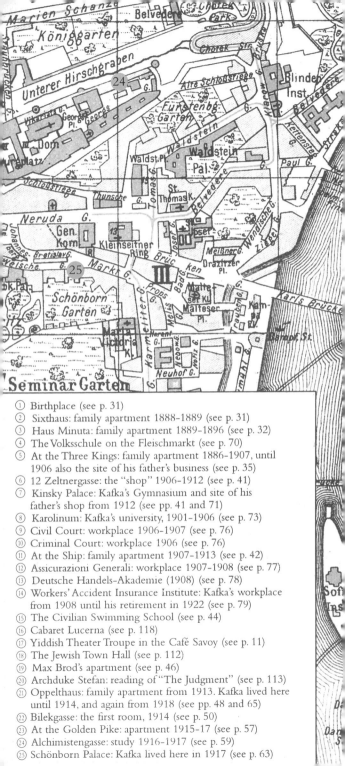